So... has died

ELAINE BROWN AND WENDY GREEN
ILLUSTRATIONS BY JOHN HAYSOM

A LION BOOK
Oxford · Batavia · Sydney

Compilation copyright © 1987 Elaine Brown and Wendy Green
This edition copyright © 1990 Lion Publishing

Published by
Lion Publishing plc
Sandy Lane West, Littlemore, Oxford, England
ISBN 0 7459 1647 3
Albatross Books Pty Ltd
PO Box 320, Sutherland, NSW 2232, Australia
ISBN 0 7324 0131 3

This material originally appeared in two books
published in 1987, under the titles *A Light Shines*
and *A Candle at Dusk*
This combined edition 1990

Acknowledgments
Quotations are reprinted by kind permission: E. M. Blaiklock,
The Bible and I, Marshall Pickering, page 31; Elizabeth Dean
Burnham, *When Your Friend is Dying*, Kingsway Publications,
page 18; Amy Carmichael, *Rose from Brier*, SPCK, page 10;
James Casson, *Dying: the Greatest Adventure of My Life*,
Christian Medical Fellowship, page, 16; Mary Craig, *Blessings*,
Hodder & Stoughton Ltd, pages 16, 32; Joni Eareckson, *A Step
Further*, Marshall Pickering and Zondervan Publishing House,
page 42; Michael Graves, *Family Magazine*, page 35; Susan
Hill, *In the Springtime of the Year*, Penguin Books Ltd, page
22; Jeanne Scheresky, *Diagnosis: Cancer*, Fleming H. Revell
Company, pages 19, 36; Katie F. Wiebe, *Alone*, Marshall
Pickering, pages 34, 43

Bible quotations from *Authorized King James Version* of the
Bible, Crown copyright; *Good News Bible*, copyright © 1966,
1971 and 1976 American Bible Society, published by the Bible
Societies/Collins; *Holy Bible, New International Version*
(British edition), copyright © 1978 New York International
Bible Society; *Revised Standard Version*, copyright © 1946
and 1952, second edition 1971, Division of Christian
Education, National Council of the Churches of Christ in the
USA; *The Living Bible*, copyright © 1971 Tyndale House
Publishers

British Library Cataloguing in Publication Data
  Green, Wendy
  Somebody I love has died.
  1. Bereavement. Christian viewpoints
  I. Title   II. Brown, Elaine
  261.5'15
  ISBN 0 7459 1647 3

Printed and bound in Spain

INTRODUCTION

The months that follow the death of someone close are like riding an emotional switchback. Relief, numbness, anger, disbelief, yearning, guilt, depression, hyper-activity pitch us from the depths to the heights, and back again.

In our pain and bewilderment we may yell at God 'Why?' 'What now?' But however deep into the darkness we go, God is there. Sometimes that knowledge comes through practical help. More often it is mediated through those who are prepared to listen and share the grief that is inevitable when someone you love has died.

This book contains just a few of the thoughts and promises which have given hope and encouragement when the way has seemed particularly bleak. May they speak God's comfort to your heart.

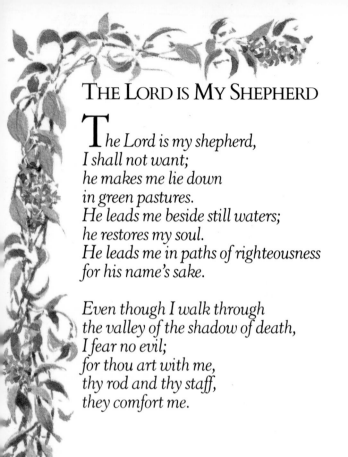

THE LORD IS MY SHEPHERD

The Lord is my shepherd,
I shall not want;
he makes me lie down
in green pastures.
He leads me beside still waters;
he restores my soul.
He leads me in paths of righteousness
for his name's sake.

Even though I walk through
the valley of the shadow of death,
I fear no evil;
for thou art with me,
thy rod and thy staff,
they comfort me.

*Thou preparest a table before me
in the presence of my enemies;
thou anointest my head with oil,
my cup overflows.
Surely goodness and mercy
shall follow me
all the days of my life;
and I shall dwell in the house
of the Lord for ever.*

Psalm 23

SOMEBODY I LOVE HAS DIED

Somebody I love has died;
they won't ever
laugh, shout,
joke, cry,
kiss, cuddle,
tease, torment,
tell me off
again.
There's an empty place at the table,
an empty space in my heart.
It's tough, Lord,
but then . . . you know.
Somebody you loved died too.

Wendy Green

No Greater Love

'Christ himself carried our sins in his body to the cross . . .'

From the first letter of Peter, chapter 2

An hour at the foot of the Cross steadies the soul as nothing else can . . . Love that loves like *that* can be trusted about this.

Amy Carmichael

A CANDLE AT DUSK

My heart is breaking, so I will
remember him . . .
The ocean depths call out to each other,
and the waterfalls of God are roaring.
They are like the waves of sorrow
with which he floods my soul.

Paraphrased from Psalm 42

HELP IN TROUBLE

Then Mary, when she came where Jesus was and saw him, fell at his feet, saying to him, 'Lord, if you had been here, my brother would not have died.' When Jesus saw her weeping, and the Jews who came with her also weeping, he was deeply moved in spirit and troubled; and he said, 'Where have you laid him?' They said to him, 'Lord, come and see.' Jesus wept. So the Jews said, 'See how much he loved him!'

The death of Lazarus, from John's Gospel, chapter 11

14

God is our refuge and strength,
an ever present help in trouble.
Therefore we will not fear . . .

'Be still, and know that I am God.'

From Psalm 46

15

Never Alone

. . . a voice inside me was saying
'There is a way through this, but
you must find it outside of yourself.
I am here, in the darkness. You are
never alone.'

Mary Craig

God will not let us go. Sometimes I feel
that I am holding by my hands to a
cliff edge — but even if I let go it is
reassuring to know I shall not slip down.

James Casson

SOMEONE WHO CARES

I've come to believe strongly that God understands our feelings. He doesn't turn his back when we are weak or hurt or depressed: he walks with us right where we are. He allows us the *dignity* to have our own feelings. And all the time, he is gently, patiently waiting to point us toward wholeness when we are ready to receive it.

Elizabeth Dean Burnham

Loving Father, we need you . . .
We are utterly helpless
today — we can only give you
this whole horrible situation.
We cannot understand why you have
allowed this to come into our
lives, but we trust you . . . I'm
asking you to stay beside us —
in us, around us . . .

Jeanne Scheresky

19

A Time for Tears

There is a season for everything,
a time for every occupation under heaven:
A time for giving birth,
a time for dying;
a time for planting,
a time for uprooting what has
been planted . . .
a time for tears,
a time for laughter;
a time for mourning,
a time for dancing.

From the book of Ecclesiastes, chapter 3

At Peace

She thought, so this is death . . . This is the body, after the spirit has left it. She put out a hand . . . the skin felt cold and smooth, like fruit. But there was peace in this room, peace and a sense of inevitability . . .

Susan Hill

D o not let your hearts be troubled. Trust in God; trust also in me. In my father's house are many rooms; if it were not so, I would have told you. I am going there to prepare a place for you . . . Peace I leave with you; my peace I give you.

Jesus' words in John's Gospel, chapter 14

HOPE RENEWED

M*y days have passed;*
my plans have failed;
my hope is gone . . .

Where is there any hope for me?
Who sees any?

If only my life could once again
be as it was when God watched over me.

From the book of Job, chapters 17 and 29

Lord, when doubts fill my mind,
when my heart is in turmoil,
quiet me and give me renewed hope . . .

From Psalm 94

DEEP WATERS

'Do not be afraid — I will save you.
I have called you by name — you are mine.
When you pass through deep waters,
I will be with you;
your troubles will not overwhelm you.
When you pass through fire,
you will not be burnt;
the hard trials that come
will not hurt you.
For I am the Lord your God . . .
you are precious to me . . .
Do not be afraid — I am with you.'

From the book of Isaiah, chapter 43

Death, be not proud,
though some have called thee
mighty and dreadful,
for thou art not so . . .

John Donne

When you sow a seed in the ground, it does not
sprout to life unless it dies. And what you sow is a
bare seed, perhaps a grain of wheat or some other
grain, not the full-bodied plant that will later grow
up. God provides that seed with the body he wishes;
he gives each seed its own proper body . . . This is
how it will be when the dead are raised to life. When
the body is buried, it is mortal; when raised, it will be
immortal. When buried, it is ugly and weak; when
raised, it will be beautiful and strong.

The apostle Paul's words,
in the first letter to the Corinthians, chapter 15

ALL IS WELL

Death is nothing at all. I have only slipped away into the next room. I am I, and you are you. Whatever we were to each other, that we still are. Call me by my old familiar name, speak to me in the easy way which you always used. Put no difference in your tone, wear no forced air of solemnity or sorrow. Laugh as we always laughed at the little jokes we enjoyed together. Pray, smile, think of me . . . Let my name be ever the household word that it always was, let it be spoken without effect, without the trace of a shadow on it. Life means all that it ever meant. It is the same as it ever was; there is unbroken continuity. Why should I be out of mind because I am out of sight? I am waiting for you, for an interval, somewhere very near, just round the corner. All is well.

Henry Scott Holland

COMFORT IN SORROW

Let us give thanks to the God and Father
of our Lord Jesus Christ, the merciful
Father, the God from whom all help comes!
He helps us in all our troubles, so that
we are able to help others who have all
kinds of troubles, using the same help
that we ourselves have received from God.
Just as we have a share in Christ's many
sufferings, so also through Christ we
share in God's great help.

From Paul's second letter to the Corinthians, chapter 1

30

A rough path is sometimes worth the treading if, in so doing, we can tread down the brambles in the path of another.

E. M. Blaiklock

Towards Compassion

It was when I had given up hope . . .
that some words I had once read
flashed into my mind with brilliant
clarity: 'Our tragedy is not that
we suffer, but that we waste suffering.
We waste the opportunity of growing
into compassion.' The words leaped
out at me, acting like a brake on
my despair, dramatically halting
my slide into madness.

Mary Craig

A Light Shines

Faith is willingness to trust God when the pieces don't fit, as well as willingness to trust when life moves along smoothly, as it will. It's not so important . . . to know why God permitted the suffering, as it is . . . to accept the tension and anguish it has created and transform it . . . Suffering must become creative.

Katie F. Wiebe

I suppose what really settled (the matter)
in my mind emotionally and spiritually
was when I finally stopped asking 'Why?'
and started asking 'For what purpose?'

Michael Graves

PROMISE OF SPRINGTIME

A bare oak tree is a symbol of a
life that is left alone, stripped of all
that is good and worthwhile and dear —
lonely, empty, and dead.

As the oak tree blooms anew each spring, so
I have faith that God will someday bring
springtime to my heart and life again.
But I never want to be so happy that I
forget these long, dark, painful days,
when I proved God's promises are true.

Jeanne Scheresky

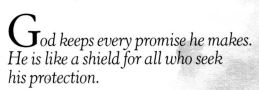

God keeps every promise he makes.
He is like a shield for all who seek
his protection.

From the book of Proverbs, chapter 30

A Future and a Hope

Life is eternal and love is immortal,
and death is only an horizon,
and an horizon is nothing
save the limit of our sight.

Bishop Brent

I *know the plans I have for you, says the
Lord, plans for welfare and not for evil; to
give you a future and a hope. Then you will
call upon me and come and pray to me, and I
will hear you. You will seek me and find me;
when you seek me with all your heart.*

From the book of Jeremiah, chapter 29

LOVE'S PARADOX

Measure thy life by loss
and not by gain,
not by the wine drunk, but
by the wine poured forth,
for Love's strength standeth in
Love's sacrifice
and he who suffers most has most to give.

Harriet Eleanor Hamilton Smith

No More Tears

When I think of heaven, I think of a time when I will be welcomed home . . . The wrongs and injustices of earth will be righted. God will measure out our tears which he has kept in his bottle, and not a single one will go unnoticed. He who holds all reasons in his hand will give us the key that makes sense out of our most senseless sufferings. And that's only the beginning.

Joni Eareckson

The absurdities, the complexities of life can be answered only with continued faith that God will put the fragments together in time. We must continue to believe he is Lord even when we cannot understand. We must always keep him in the picture.

Hope is always more important than happiness.

Katie F. Wiebe

Death is No More

Then I saw a new heaven and a new earth.
The first heaven and the first earth
disappeared and the sea vanished.

I heard a loud voice speaking:
'Now God's home is with mankind!
He will live with them,
and they shall be his people.
God himself will be with them,
and he will be their God.
He will wipe away all tears from their eyes.
There will be no more death,
no more grief or crying or pain.
The old things have disappeared.'

From the book of Revelation, chapter 21